From Memories *to* Manuscript

The Five-Step Method of Writing Your Life Story

Joan R. Neubauer

Library of Congress Cataloging-in-Publication Data

Neubauer, Joan R.
    From memories to manuscript : the five step method of
writing your life story life story/Joan R. Neubauer.
        p.   cm.
    Includes bibliographical references
    ISBN 0-916489-56.6
    1. Autobiography-Authorship.   I. Title.
CT25.N49   1994
808'.06692-dc20   93-43942

Published by Ancestry® Publishing,
an imprint of MyFamily.com, Inc.

P.O. Box 990
Orem UT 84059
www.myfamily.com

First printing 1994
10 9 8 7 6 5 4 3

Printed in Canada

*This book
is dedicated to
my husband
and best friend,
Steve, as we make
new memories for
our future.*

CONTENTS

*F*ought to write a book." How many times have you heard people say that? Perhaps you've even said it a time or two. As a writer, I've heard it countless times. Everyone has a story to tell. Everyone feels that his or her autobiography or the story of his or her town, company, church, or organization would make a great book. And they're right. You as an individual are important. Your town or organization is important. The things you know have value, and the lessons you have learned are priceless. Now you have come to a crossroads and feel it is time to write the story you know is waiting to be told.

The reasons for writing such a book, an autobiography, are as varied as there are stories to tell, and each is valid, for they all come from deep within the heart. Some people record their life stories to comply with a basic tenet of their religion. For others, writing an autobiography is an attempt to "tell it like it really was." But the bottom line for most individuals is that they recognize that such a book enables them to leave a more complete legacy.

As others read your autobiography they will come to know you in a way that would not have been possible otherwise. You can make people and places come alive so that your reader can experience the sweetness of your successes and the sorrow of your failures.

In an autobiography, your own words can give your children and grandchildren the chance to see you in a new light. They will realize that you were a child once yourself when they read how you got caught sliding down the banister at school, or broke a window playing baseball.

So, you want to write a book? Think of this as your opportunity to tell a story as it has never before been told. The project will require time and dedication, but the finished product will be of great value in years to come. This is your chance to tell a story that will be worth more than any measure of money, for it is a dream fulfilled. It is part of you. It is one of a kind.

INTRODUCTION

Congratulations! You've made the decision to undertake a great adventure, to write the book you always said you would. The story is waiting within you—waiting to be written—but you don't where to start.

From Memories to Manuscript is a handbook written to help you write a quality autobiography that others will want to read. Each of the five sections describes a step that will lead you through the process professionals use when writing, and each step is discussed in detail.

And while this all sounds very systematic, the book is designed with you as an individual in mind. The method described will assist you in looking at your project in smaller, more manageable pieces, and will help you accomplish this noble goal you have set for yourself. Here is your opportunity to relive cherished memories, laugh at the silly situations, and reflect upon those things that have made a difference in your life. Now is the time to remember those who came before you and others who have enriched your life as you travelled life's road together for a time. With the written word comes power and authority. You can use it to reminisce with those who have known you for years and share how things really happened with those who come later.

Try to follow this guide step by step. Take as much time as you need. Work on your autobiography every day, even if for just a few minutes; this will help to keep you involved with the project, and you will be more likely to finish it.

Keep track of the number of hours you spend on the book—it's always a great way to impress yourself!

With that in mind, are you ready? Good! Together, let us go adventuring...

Step 1

Research

STEP I: RESEARCH

𝓕t's time to get started. Professional writers know that before they write a single word they must have all their facts in hand. And, believe it or not, even though you're writing your own life story you will have to do some research.

GATHERING INFORMATION

That research may mean talking with people about times past, reliving memories with friends, or looking through old photo albums. You may find yourself reviewing dusty old record books in your church library or the cellar archives of city hall. In some cases, you may even have to go to the library for some facts and figures. Gather all the information you can find or recall.

Some cities and towns have whole libraries or societies dedicated to genealogy or local history. The Church of Jesus Christ of Latter-day Saints also generously makes its vast genealogical resources available to the public at its local Family History Centers. If you live near any of these resources, take advantage of what they have to offer.

In any case, become well acquainted with the resources available in your area and take advantage of them. The information will serve to make a more informative and interesting book.

RECORDING WHAT YOU FIND

As you gather information, avoid recording facts on little slips of paper. They tend to get lost. Instead, I recommend you use one of two methods. The first requires a three-ring notebook and lined filler paper. Whenever you remember something about your school days in elementary school, for example, record it on a single page. Date it if at all possible. The great thing about this system is that you can use as many sheets as you need. When you're done, you can manipulate the pages to determine their proper order. This method not only helps in future organization, but prevents the loss of valuable facts.

The second system uses 3 by 5-inch index cards. It's much the same as the notebook method, in that you record one piece of information on each card. Again, the cards are easy to manipulate, are all the same size, and can be held together neatly with a rubber band. The added plus with the card method is that you can slip them easily into your pocket or purse to take to the library or someone's house to record information.

Don't feel you must commit to either one system or the other from the beginning of this process. Instead, experiment for a short time to determine what works best for you. If you like to write a lot, the notebook might serve you better. If you prefer taking shorter notes, the index cards might work to your advantage. Whatever the case, try each for a week or two. You'll develop a preference very quickly. At that point, either buy yourself a few reams of paper or several packs of cards so that you'll have plenty of materials on hand.

At the end of your research, you will probably have more stacks of cards or pages of information than you ever thought you'd want. Take heart; this is what every writer experiences after a period of research. But don't give in to the temptation to use every piece of information you've gathered. Don't feel you must recount every experience or event; it would be a monumental task, and the resulting volume would probably be several feet thick. At the proper time, you'll choose which bits and pieces of information to use in the book and which ones just to file away.

REMEMBERING THE FACTS

This is the time to write down what you remember. The pages that follow present questions that will help jog your memory. Remember, these questions are only a beginning; you would do well to continue asking yourself similar questions of your own.

- Where and when were you born?

- Were you born under unusual circumstances—was there a blizzard outside at the time? Did a significant historical event occur on that day?

- What are the names of your parents? Include your mother's maiden name, middle names, nicknames family members may have had for them, or names they had for each other.

- What are the names, nicknames, birth dates of your brothers and sisters?

- Where did you live when you were growing up?

- Did you ever move? If so, was it hard to leave the old place behind? Was it easy to adjust to the new place?

- Who were your best friends as a child? Why were they your best friends? How long did these friendships last? Do any of them continue today?

- What schools did you attend?
- Did you participate in athletic activities? If so, what were they?

- Who were your coaches?

- Who were your teammates?

- Who were your favorite teachers?

- Did any of your teachers influence your life in some positive way?

- What were your favorite subjects in school?

- Do you have any special memories of friends or events from school?

- How did your family celebrate birthdays? Did you have a party every year? Was there a special celebration?

- When did you graduate from high school? College? Graduate school? Other schools?

- What kinds of music did you like?

- What was your favorite movie?

- Who were your favorite movie stars?

- Were there any special pieces of furniture in your house or unique features of your home as you were growing up? Can you tell a memorable story about any of them?

- Did your family travel much?

- Where did your family vacation? What was your favorite vacation spot?

- What was your first job?

- If you served in the military, what branch of the service were you in?

- When and where did you serve? What was your rank? Who were your buddies?

- Do you recall any memorable stories?

- If you are or have been married, when and where did you meet your spouse(s)?

- What was your first impression of your spouse(s) when you met?

- Do you have any special memories of the time you were courting?

- If you have children, when and where were they born?

- What jobs have you held and during which years? Did you receive any promotions?

- What places have you lived and when?

- Do you remember any special birthday celebrations? Anniversaries?

- Do you recall any other special events?

- Have you experienced the loss of loved ones?

You'll notice that using this technique is almost like creating a character for a book, and in a sense you are. You're recreating yourself on paper in order to tell your story. You are a real person with likes, dislikes, good qualities, and failings, and you want to convey all those things to your reader.

Remember that the questions suggested above are just that—suggestions to get you started and going in the right direction. You'll be surprised at how one question leads to another, and how one bit of information sheds light on another fact. It's almost like being a detective. If other questions and memories come to mind, by all means address them.

When answering the questions, be as descriptive as possible. Include such details as the time of year, the appearance of your surroundings, a particular perfume in the air, or a song that may have been playing in the background.

OTHER RESOURCES

Other tools you might use to jog your memory are old photo albums, home movies, and videos. You may have a pressed rose hidden away in your family Bible or dictionary—and every time you see it, your memory takes you back to a particular time and place. It's almost as if you were reliving the moment. Use all of those things to help you recall certain events, names, and people you may otherwise have forgotten. And don't hesitate to dig out those old records and tapes.

Music has a wonderful way of bringing memories alive. Can you remember the song the organ played as you marched down the aisle at your wedding? Chances are that, as you replay the song in your memory, you'll also see the faces of the people who came to celebrate with you.

Smell, too, evokes powerful recollections. Let me share a personal example with you. I remember summer nights when my mother and I would walk to my aunt's house two blocks away. While my mother and aunt rocked on the front porch and talked, my cousin and I sat on the sidewalk or played games with shadows cast by the street lights. On those nights the sweet scent of honeysuckle filled the air and came to us on soft breezes from across the street. To this day, whenever I recognize that lovely fragrance, my mind goes back to those nights, and I have to smile. That's what I mean by sensory descriptions. Write them down. Those memories are priceless.

For your own convenience, try to keep things in chronological order as much as possible. This will help you later when you begin to organize all the information you've gathered. If you choose to arrange your book or sections in your book chronologically (see step two), dates will be very important, and you will want to date events whenever you can. In cases where you cannot remember an exact date, try to recall if it came before or after other events. For example, ask yourself, "Did this happen before or after Mary got married? If it happened afterward, did it happen before Bill went to college?" This is a wonderful method for dating events. It will not be as exact as knowing that an event happened on July 29, 1952, but it will be close enough for you to put it in its proper place in the book.

Also, keep a notebook handy at all times. Whenever a name, event, or date flashes into your mind, write it down, and then be sure to transfer the information to your larger notebook or file cards so the information isn't lost.

Tape recorders are also useful. If you recall a particular memory you'd like to include in your book, simply press the record button and speak into the microphone. You may be surprised at how much you'll remember once you start talking. A microcassette recorder that fits into your pocket or purse can be a good yet inexpensive investment.

Some people record their entire life stories on tape, and then transcribe the tapes (or have someone do it for them) and bind the results into a book. This would be great if you remembered everything in the exact order you'd like to have it appear in the book. However, this rarely happens. Once the tapes are transcribed, there usually is a great deal of organizational work to be done (though word-processing software makes the task much easier).

My advice is to use a tape recorder as a method to jog your memory or to record isolated events to be included in the book, and then write them down. All those memories are too precious to lose.

Step 2
Organize

STEP II: ORGANIZE

*N*ow that you've completed your research and gathered the information you need for your book, you must organize it. You're probably wondering just what you're going to do with those facts. You're also probably wondering whatever came over you in the first place to think you could possibly write this book.

Let me tell you that what you have achieved thus far is marvelous. I know it's easy to become discouraged when things don't go as you expect them to. In fact, I can almost promise you that, during this process of writing your autobiography, you will experience frustration—but that's normal. At some point, all writers feel that way, and I think it has something to do with feeling that you've lost control of the project. But take heart, because you haven't. Move on, and never lose sight of your goal, a completed book. You must not look upon this project as a whole, but in terms of smaller, more manageable bits. That makes the job less overwhelming and enables you to keep control.

Let's get specific. When writing your autobiography, you can begin by organizing your story through milestones in your life such as graduations, weddings, the birth of children, or job changes. These are the things that have probably had the most influence on your life; thus, you can build other events around them.

Obviously you came from somewhere, so if you'd like to include a small bit of information about your family history in the beginning, that might be a good idea. Begin with a family story or two, tell where your ancestors came from, what they did for a living, and how many children they had. Then, move into your own story.

CREATING A TIMELINE

An easy way to organize all this is with a timeline. This is a horizontal line drawn across a page. It represents the span of a life from birth to the present day (or any other length of time you wish to chronicle). For example, take the card or sheet of paper that says you were born on May 28, 1930. Write that event on your time-line. The next date in your stack of information says, "Started school in September 1935." Move to the right on the timeline, make a vertical mark for 1935, and record that you began school. Continue in that way until you've accounted for all the information you've gathered. Below is a sample:

1930	1935	1948
Born	Started School	Graduated High School

This example is very simple; your timeline will be more detailed. Don't feel you must limit yourself to a standard 8 1/2 by 11-inch sheet of paper. Use as much paper or as large a sheet as you need. Fan-fold computer paper works very well because you can use as long a length as you like. Tack it up on a wall and add dates and events whenever you think of them.

While there is no need to record the name of every person who has crossed your path, be sure to include the important or influential names, dates, and places. It will make your job of actually writing the book so much easier. But don't feel that just because a person's name appears on your timeline the person must be included in your book. When the time comes to write the book, you will make the decision not to relate certain instances from your life because they serve no real purpose in your book. But we'll discuss this issue in more depth later. Right now, you must put everything in its proper place on your timeline.

ARRANGING THE FACTS

When your timeline is complete, you may organize your information in two different ways. The first, and most popular, method of arrangement is chronological; the second method arranges information according to subject.

THE CHRONOLOGICAL APPROACH

I'll describe the chronological approach first. With this method, your story proceeds from one event to the next in the sequence in which they occurred, regardless of topic. Thus, in one chapter you may tell about your marriage, the birth of your first child, buying your first house, and your first job promotion. The events are bound together by the fact that they all occurred within a given time period.

Using this method, you will break the events of your life into segments of about ten years, or whatever makes the most sense. Below is an example:

Chapter 1:	1920-1930
Chapter 2:	1930-1940
Chapter 3:	1940-1950
Chapter 4:	1950-1955
Chapter 5:	1955-1960
Chapter 6:	1960-1970
Chapter 7:	1970-1980
Chapter 8:	1980-1990
Chapter 9:	1990-present

If you choose, you may also give a title to each chapter, such as "Chapter 1, Early Childhood." This will help you organize your information, as well as give you the layout of your book.

THE TOPICAL APPROACH

The second method is to arrange your information according to topic. This may be appropriate for periods in which many things were happening in your life simultaneously. For example, during the early years of your marriage, things may have been difficult financially. In order to make ends meet, you may have worked at two or three jobs. Keeping track of those jobs, salary, bosses, events, and even amusing stories about co-workers, might prove difficult when placed in the context of your marriage and growing family. In that case, separate the employment stories from family stories. There will be some overlap, but it will be easier for your readers to keep things straight in their minds. An example follows:

Chapter 1: Early Childhood (1930-1940)
Chapter 2: School Days (1935-1942)
Chapter 3: Adolescence (1943-1948)
Chapter 4: Friends (1943-1948)
Chapter 5: College (1948-1952)
Chapter 6: Marriage and Family (1952-1962)
Chapter 7: Employment (1952-1965)
Chapter 8: Family Stories (1962-1992)
Chapter 9: Retirement (1992-present)

As you can see, the chapters are still arranged chronologically, but each deals with a specific topic. Sometimes a combination of the two methods works best. Keep it chronological whenever possible. However, when things get too hectic, change to the topical method. It can prevent some confusion.

CREATING AN OUTLINE

After you've developed the general organization of your book by using the approaches described above, develop each chapter in more detail by creating an outline. Let's use the preceding list of chapters as an example to show you how. Since there are nine chapters, use nine cards or sheets of paper and write a chapter number, title, and date on each one. Place them in order, left to right, on a large surface such as a table, counter, or the floor. Next, place each card or sheet in a pile below the appropriate heading, and then sort the cards or sheets into the proper order. When you've finished, you're ready to create your outline, line by line, in a very detailed manner. Below is a condensed example for Chapter 1:

Chapter 1

Born in Wichita, Kansas, in April 1930 to mother Ann, father John.

> Father, age 30, was a journalist. Mother, age 26, helped at her father's hardware store.

> I had a sister, Virginia, age 4, and a brother, Alan, age 2.

Effects of Great Depression dominated life in the United States at this time.

> In 1936, father lost his job at local newspaper.
> In 1937, my brother took a job selling newspapers. I helped him.

> In 1939, family moved to California when father found work in the aviation industry there.

Your outline will probably be much more extensive than this example, but the point of creating an outline is clear: you are creating the framework of your autobiography by writing down the details and ordering them as they relate to one another.

Take a good look at the information you've compiled and where you've placed it in your outline. Before you go on to the next step, be sure the information is well-organized and easy-to-follow. Have you chosen the right method to organize your information? Does it make your story easy-to-follow? Always keep the reader in mind, and make sure the events flow logically from one to the other. Don't feel you must cram everything into nine or ten chapters; there might be too much information. Fifteen or twenty chapters might work better for you. Now is the time to expand or condense the information.

If anything is out of sequence, now is the time to rearrange. Check one last time to see that all names, dates, and places are correct. Have you included all the stories you'd like to tell? If something occurs to you later as you write the book, it should be easy enough to add. However, for your own convenience, everything should be ready to go at this time. If so, reward yourself with a special treat. You've done well and you're ready to go on to the next step.

Step 3
Write

STEP III: WRITE

S mile! You have accomplished a great deal and are ready to proceed with the next step—writing. The research and outlining are done, and it's time to tell your story as you've been wanting to do for so long.

GETTING TO THE PURPOSE

If you have access to a personal computer and word-processing software, your task will be easier. Such technology allows you to manipulate information with a keystroke. Most word-processing software also offers you the ability to check your spelling, and some programs will even check your grammar. Both are welcome helps when working on such a project. However, be aware that, as helpful as spellcheckers and grammar checkers are, they are not infallible. Certain incorrect usages may escape them. For example, a spellchecker will not correct the improper use of "there" in place of "their" or vice versa.

If you are handwriting your manuscript, don't feel handicapped—a computer is not required to write a book. Remember, Shakespeare penned some of the greatest works of all time by hand.

As you write, don't worry if what you produce doesn't sound polished. Most professional writers experience the same thing. Keep writing. Rarely does anything elegant appear on paper after the first writing. Most writers edit their work several times before producing a product good enough to submit for publication. At this point, the important thing is to write the words and tell the story. Keep telling yourself that, in years to come, friends and relatives will be grateful that you did.

Follow your outline from point to point. Reward yourself with a big check mark and a pat on the back after you complete each section. However, don't feel that the outline is inflexible. If you feel that adding an event here or there will enhance your story, then by all means add it in the appropriate place. After all, you want your book to be as complete as possible. On the other hand, if a particular item seems mundane, uneventful, or has no real significance in the story, then don't use it. Resist the temptation to include every little detail.

KNOWING WHAT TO INCLUDE

How do you determine which stories to include and which ones to cut? Ask yourself a few guiding questions:

1. Does this tell the reader something important about me and my life? If you include a particular story, be sure the reader comes away with a new understanding about you.

2. Is it important for the reader to know that on nights I couldn't sleep past four o'clock in the morning I got out of bed and started ironing? This could be a fine way to demonstrate that you are a hard worker. But be careful—one or two such stories are plenty. Don't give a litany of them. It could get boring for both you and the reader.

3. Is it important that the reader understand why I went into business for myself or accomplished something else? If there were unusual circumstances leading up to going into business or becoming a salesman, that would be fine to include. Otherwise, start with the intention of simply saying "This is what happened..."

4. Will this story move the book along or bog it down? If the reader will learn something new, or if the inclusion of a particular story will quicken the pace, then include it. Otherwise, leave it out.

5. Must I include every person I ever met and every event of my life? Absolutely not. You will, however, want to include those people who have been important to you for one reason or another. For instance, perhaps someone influenced you a great deal in your business and as a result you were successful. Maybe you modeled your life after a favorite uncle. Whatever the case, use your judgement, and then show how they made a difference in your life.

ACCENTUATING THE DETAILS

As you write, also remember to set the mood. Perhaps tell what time of year it was, or that you can still remember the smell of the gardenias in the corsage you wore to your first dance. Use one or two of the five senses in each scene. Don't rely entirely on what you saw. Describe the music you heard, or how it felt the first time you held hands, or that the punch tasted like someone added too much sugar. These details are all important in bringing the scene alive. Remember, particulars make the difference between competent writing and wonderful writing.

In addition to setting the scene and making use of the five senses, you should also include dialogue whenever possible. Conversation has a way of drawing readers into a book and keeping interest high. Dialogue also gives your readers a sense of "being there," something every writer wishes to accomplish.

Another consideration in writing your autobiography needs to be your point of view. In other words, since this is an autobiography, you should write it in the first person: use the pronoun "I" when referring to yourself. However, I caution you about overusing that particular pronoun, especially when beginning sentences. Try to be creative and come up with alternatives.

Work on your book a little each day, even if it is only for fifteen minutes. If you can spend an hour or two, then so much the better. But just by producing one page a day, at the end of a year you'll have a book that is three-hundred and sixty-five pages long. Any professional writer will tell you that the trick to writing is to write something every day.

Yes, you will experience frustration from time to time. That is to be expected with any writing project. Perhaps when that happens, it's best to put the book away for an hour or so. Take a walk. Have a cup of tea. Phone a friend. You will be surprised at how refreshed you will be when you return to writing.

Step 4
Edit

When you have finished writing, put the book aside for a few days or a week. This is a practice professionals use to detach themselves from their work before they edit it. Detachment and objectivity are both very important when editing. You must be able to look at a paragraph or a sentence objectively to decide if it is necessary or if it can be improved.

POLISHING THE PROSE

This is the time to polish your writing and make it professional. You may have to edit the book two or three times or more; each time, you will see things that need to be changed. Don't be discouraged. This is a common step in all writing. Many authors completely revise a book several times before they are satisfied with it.

As you read your words, you may also discover that your writing is not as strong as that of your favorite author. There are some "tricks of the trade" that can make your writing better as you edit. These are techniques that professionals use to make their writing better, stronger, and more direct. Example sentences are followed by the revised version directly below.

TRICKS OF THE TRADE

1. Look for verbs that end in "ing." If possible, change them to the simple past tense—that is, verbs that end with "d" or "ed." These simple verbs add power and clarity to your writing.

Example: Walking into the room, Jack saw Betsy sitting by the fireplace.

Revised: Jack walked into the room where Betsy sat by the fireplace.

2. Look for verbs that are part of the verb "to be," such as *am, is, are, was, were,* and *been.* Also look for auxiliary or helping verbs such as *have, had,* and *has.* These verbs make your writing passive. Try to use active, past tense verbs to make your writing more definite, exciting, and stronger.

Example: We were waiting for the bus.

Revised: We waited for the bus.

3. Look for adjectives and adverbs. Do not overuse them, and don't use them in long strings. Make your verbs do the work for you.

Example: Julie walked quickly through the large, popular, lush, sunlit city park.

Revised: Julie jogged through the popular city park. She noticed how the bright sunlight accentuated the lush foliage.

4. Avoid the use of unnecessary words. If one word will do the job of two, or three, or more, use it.

Example: Stephen dropped the plate to the floor.

Revised: Stephen dropped the plate.

Of course it fell to the floor! If he had dropped the plate on a couch, chair, or elsewhere, you would mention where it landed.

5. Be descriptive. Show the reader what you are talking about. It is not enough to simply tell.

Example: Regina, the truck driver's beautiful daughter, had long black hair.

Revised: You could imagine Regina as a fairy-tale princess, locked in a tower, her long black hair trailing to the ground like a thick rope.

6. Avoid long, drawn-out sentences that string many thoughts together. Many times it is much more efficient to break a long sentence into two sentences; it is also easier for the reader to understand.

Example: The way I found out about the fire was when Bill told me about the fire trucks going down his street with their sirens blaring in the early hours this morning.

Revised: Bill told me about the fire. He said the fire trucks rushed down his street early this morning.

7. Try to vary your vocabulary. Don't use the same word too often. Have a good dictionary and thesaurus on hand to help you.

As an example, here are a few alternatives for the simple verb "jump": *bound, hop, leap, vault, catapult.* See how much more interesting your writing becomes with the use of such alternatives.

Be sure to incorporate these methods in your own writing whenever you can, but don't forget to use description in the process. While these techniques are useful, use them only as a guide. If you allow yourself to be creative, you'll surprise yourself with your writing ability. Below is one last example of what can be done with two simple sentences to make them more exciting.

Example: In 1775, Bristol, Pennsylvania was a very busy trading town. There were many stores and much activity.

Revised: The market was alive, singing with the daily activities of the townspeople. Women travelled from shop to stall, carrying baskets overflowing with the abundance of the market. Sounds from the smithy's hammer rose above the din in the street, and the clang of iron on iron reaffirmed the normalcy of life.

Now, take a good look at your own work as objectively as possible and make whatever corrections, additions, or deletions you feel would make it better. If you don't feel comfortable with the editing process, it might help to have someone else read your work and edit it for you. Professional writers agree that it's always good to have a second opinion of your work.

If you find yourself having difficulty with the organization, writing, or editing of your autobiography, you should know that help is available. First, there are a number of books on the market that give good, practical advice on grammar and style, and specifically on writing your autobiography. Most of them are available in your local public library or through inter-library loan. For your convenience I have included a bibliography at the back of this guide. These are by no means the only books you can choose from, but they're a good start.

Second, you can contact a local writers' group and ask for such help. The amount you pay them, of course, depends on how little or how much they have to do for you. Such requests are welcomed by writers' group members.

I have helped a number of people from all walks of life to write their autobiographies. They are from all social and economic backgrounds and have an almost limitless number of stories to tell, but they have one thing in common: they want to leave a unique legacy for the future, .and no one can say that an autobiography isn't truly unique. Now, it's your turn.

Step 5

Print and Publish

STEP V: PRINT & PUBLISH

Congratulate yourself. You have now completed four of the five steps in writing your book. It is your story as only you can tell it, and you have presented it as only you can. Now what do you do with it? You have a number of options, depending on how you have produced your book.

CREATING THE FINAL PRODUCT

If your manuscript is handwritten, you might want to type it yourself or hire someone to do it for you. A more efficient way is to have someone enter it into a computer, save it to a diskette, and print a copy for you. Once it's on diskette, you can have it formatted in book form (through typesetting or desktop publishing) for a nominal fee. This process will facilitate publishing additional copies.

If you have written your book on a computer using word-processing software, you may also have the software to typeset it yourself, or you can take your diskette to someone who can. Clearly, already having your manuscript on a diskette will save you money if you decide to have your story typeset.

At this point, if you want only a few copies, it is very inexpensive and little trouble to make those copies using a photocopy machine. Depending on the number of pages, you can then bind them yourself using report folders or spiral binders, or you can have them bound at a print shop. If, however, you want more than ten or twenty copies, you would be wise to go to a duplicating service or printer to have them reproduced.

Duplicating services typically reproduce documents using photocopy machines, and they can produce excellent results. Often only an expert can tell the difference between a copy that came from one of these copiers and one that came from a printer's press. The advantage of a copier-produced book is that it is less expensive.However, if you want more than a few hundred copies, a printer can give you comparable prices and often a wider variety of services. Printers use more traditional ink presses and can give you the highest-quality results. Shop around for the best quality at the best price.

If you'd like a few bound copies as keepsakes for special people, there are binderies that will bind small quantities of books. Prices for each 8 1/2 by 11-inch bound volume vary from about $25 for imitation leather to $100 for real leather. Such binderies can provide you with attractive embossed covers in various colors.

Again, this is your book and your decision to make. But now that your book is written, finish the job. Print it or publish it in some form. Maybe you wrote your story to fulfill a dream, leave a more complete legacy, or simply to "tell it like it really was." Whatever your reason, you've come this far. Don't stop short of your goal!

BIBLIOGRAPHY

Baker, Russell, and William Knowlton Zinsser. *Inventing the Truth: The Art and Craft of Memoirs.* Boston: Houghton Mifflin, 1987.
This is a how-to instructional text that sets guidelines for what to include and what to exclude when writing a memoir.

Banks, Keith E. *How To Write Your Personal and Family History.* 2d ed. Bowie, Md.:Heritage Books, 1989.
This book deals not only with writing the autobiography, but family history and genealogy research as well. While it concerns itself with gathering and recording information from the past, it also deals with preserving contemporary documents and journal writing as legacies for future generations.

Bradbury, Ray. *Zen in the Art of Writing: Essays on Writing and Creativity.* Santa Barbara, Calif.: Joshua Odell Editions, 1989.
The well-known science fiction writer presents a different philosophical viewpoint regarding creativity, how to tap into it, and how to use it to your advantage.

Daniel, Lois. *How to Write Your Own Life Story: A Step By Step Guide for the Non-professional Writer.* Chicago: Chicago Review Press, 1985.
This is a basic text for the non-writer that describes the process of writing your autobiography. It contains valuable examples.

Dixon, Janice T., and Dora D. Flack. *Preserving Your Past: A Painless Guide to Writing Your Autobiography and Family History.* Garden City, N.Y.: Doubleday, 1977.
Dixon's book is a reader-friendly guide to the process of writing an autobiography and conducting genealogy research.

Goldberg, Natalie. *Wild Mind.* New York: Bantam Books, 1990.
Writing Down the Bones. Boston: Shambhala, 1986.
Both of Natalie Goldberg's books contain excellent writing exercises to get your creative juices flowing. They're wonderful as warm-ups to put you in the right mood before working on your project.

Gouldrup, Lawrence P. *Writing the Family Narrative.* Salt Lake City: Ancestry, 1989.
An accompanying workbook is also available. This is an informative, practical workbook designed to jog your memory. It is filled with examples and helpful hints to lead you through the writing process.

Kelsch, Mary Lynn, and Thomas Kelsch. *Writing Effectively: A Practical Guide.* Englewood Cliffs, N.J.: Prentice Hall, 1981.
Writing Effectively provides specific tips to strengthen your writing. It includes such subjects as tone, dialogue, narration, and better expression of ideas.

Selling, Bernard. *Writing from Within: A Step By Step Guide to Writing Your Life's Stories.* Claremont, Calif.: Hunter House, 1988.
This book helps you tap into your memories and guides you to record them most effectively.

Strunk, William Jr., and E. B. White. *The Elements of Style*. 3d ed. New York: Macmillan Publishing Co., 1979.
The Elements of Style has become a standard regarding grammar and usage. It is simple to understand and gives good examples to demonstrate each point.

Thomas, Frank P, *How To Write the Story of your Life*. Cincinnati, Ohio: Writer's Digest Books, 1984.
Thomas has written a well-thought.out guide to writing the autobiography using "memory sparkers," outlines, and free-association skills. He offers many points of departure and pages of questions to get you started.

Zinsser, William Knowlton. *On Writing Well. An Informal Guide to Writing Nonfiction*. 2d ed. New York: Harper and Row, 1980.
In this book, Zinsser presents practical suggestions to improve your writing. It's easy to read and offers good examples.
Writing with a Word Processor. New York: Harper and Row, 1983. Zinsser manages to simplify what some regard as mystifying. He gets past the intimidation of high-tech equipment and gives the reader the means to become comfortable with the new technology.

ABOUT THE AUTHOR

$\mathcal{J}$oan R. Neubauer established herself as a freelance writer in 1987 and has since sold a variety of articles to both regional and national publications. A graduate of West Chester University in Pennsylvania, Joan taught Spanish and English-As-A-Second-Language for a number of years before pursuing a second career as a writer.

In 1990, she founded Word Wright International as a copywriting firm to serve the writing needs of Houston's business community. However, Joan soon recognized a different need and her company now specializes in helping people write their life stories.

On the subject of autobiographies, Joan says: "They are by far the most enthralling adventures I've had as a writer and they make me wonder how many other wonderful stories there are to tell."

In addition to writing, she now teaches classes, conducts workshops, and frequently addresses groups where she educates her audiences as a businesswoman, educator, and writer.